*I've learned that to heal we must forgive the devil.
It's that simple.*

# Born to Feel a Brain

By: Mighty Angel

# CONTENTS

Chapter 1:   Born to feel a brain

Chapter 2:   I don't like my favorite thing anymore?

Chapter 3:   A species driven by Pain?

Chapter 4:   Beware the Feelings Bitch

Chapter 5:   MONEY

Chapter 6:   "Dis-Orders" from the brain

Chapter 7:   So you wanna make a baby?

Chapter 8:   "Destiny"  Has your life already been written?

Chapter 9:   Don't lie to me!

Chapter 10:  Judge-less

Chapter 11:  Why the Hell does that feel good, brain?

Chapter 12:  Of course there's a Hell

Chapter 13:  Stealing Heaven

I wrote this book to share a very simple yet life-changing message: we're all the same, born to feel a brain.

# CHAPTER 1

## Born to feel a brain

On your mark, get set, go!

Fact: Roughly the same ratios of people are raped, robbed, kidnapped and killed every single year like clockwork.

Fact: Humans create statistics that are so similar each year we can actually **predict the future** and foretell how many of us are going to be raped, robbed, kidnapped and killed in the years to come.

My people: We shouldn't be able to know how many of us are going to be raped, robbed, kidnapped and killed every single year, as if we were on some sort of factory conveyor belt—unless we were meant to stop it.

**It's time for us to know the truth about this world and the brains we've been forced into upon entering it.**

We humans exist within brains that are capable of hurting us when they're not stimulated, which means we get punished every time our brains are not entertained.

Fact: Our brains will hurt us with sensations of boredom just for having to sit in one spot for too long, but it doesn't end there because if left "untreated," we can go from feeling bored to feeling desperate, depraved and even insane.

Fact: Lock a person up in isolation (solitary confinement) for more than three days and they can start to "lose their mind."

This is why we humans (as a whole) engage in every activity imaginable that promises to stimulate our brains—it doesn't matter how crazy, immoral, or dangerous it is!

Dog-fighting, vandalism, overeating, drug abuse, theft, adultery, prostitution, kidnapping, rape, murder, war, terrorism, you name it; we do it! It's what's been #trending in this world since the beginning of time.

If you take away a child's game, the child cries. The tears come from pain, and all pain comes from the brain. Thus making the message clear: our brains hurt us for stimulation.

A landmark study at Harvard and Virginia Universities found that humans would rather experience physical pain over fifteen minutes of boredom.

Which means humans would rather be at war than at peace, which makes perfect sense considering humans have been at war since the beginning of time.

World wars, civil wars, race wars, wars between rival gangs, wars between siblings, wars between spouses, and now televised wars between housewives.

An idle brain causes pain, which causes us to hurt each other, and even ourselves for stimulation! Teasing, bullying, beating, cutting, intoxicating, and even killing, which proves:

## Human suffering stimulates the human brain

This is why people cheered when witnessing slaves being mutilated in gladiator contests, decapitated in guillotines, hung, stoned, burned, and buried alive...our species actually gave standing ovations for this stuff.

Evil is the reaction of pain from the brain and we humans are made to feel pain just for having to sit in one spot for too long.

**This is the human condition—the dilemma that is behind the reason why babies cry for a toy and adults overdose from drugs, kill for money, and live obese.**

We humans are "instinctive" creatures, which means we have "built-in" urges and are driven by the sensations of our inherited brains, and these sensations are what determine our perspective and therefore our reality.

This is the reason why our dreams "feel so real" and why a person can experience an orgasm while dreaming without any physical contact whatsoever. It's because all feelings (whether emotional or physical) come from the brain, and these sensations are what determine our reality, not the physical world around us!

Allow me to explain:

Most humans have at least five senses. These are: seeing, hearing, smelling, touching, and tasting.

However, what we need to understand is that these senses work directly for the brain, not us! Their purpose is to deliver raw information for the brain to process, not you!

**You're the third party**, the last to receive information, which means everything you encounter in life is first filtered by your brain, then translated to you as a feeling you do not control and these feelings (sensations) are what determine our reality.

For example, if three "normal-looking" guys were to see an attractive woman crossing their path, here are just a few examples of what they might be <u>forced to feel</u>:

- The first guy might be <u>forced to feel</u> turned-on by the attractive woman and want to get with her sexually.

- The second guy might be <u>forced to feel</u> jealous of the attractive woman, wishing he too could walk the streets as a confident, sexy woman in heels.

- And the third guy might be <u>forced to feel</u> a desire to kill the attractive woman, believing he must rid the world of evildoers (temptresses).

We humans are **forced to feel** something about everything we encounter in life, and these feelings are what determine our reality, under the command of a brain that may make us feel whatever we don't want. From natural-born serial killers to natural-born caretakers, it's what's in our genes!

**The process of our brains experiencing matter from the world and releasing random chemical sensations onto us as a consequence has absolutely nothing to do with us!**

Helping us to understand that:

- Not all "perverts" want to masturbate in the shadows.
- Not all homosexuals want to come out of the closet.
- Not all transgender people want to transition.
- Not all drug addicts want to overdose and die.
- Not all compulsive eaters want to be obese.
- Not all pedophiles want to rape children.
- Not all compulsive shoppers want to be bankrupt.
- Not all necrophilia's want to dig up corpses for sex.
- Not all serial killers want to murder innocent people.

**Yet these are the sorts of things billions of humans are <u>forced to feel</u> (manufactured to feel) every single day from a "fixed" brain, which arguably, just may mean that our entire human experience is fixed, as we continue to create the same worldly statistics every single year like clockwork!**

To be human is to step into a chemical field of sensations that were established thousands of years ago, indebted to the insatiable needs and wants of a temperamental brain that is completely out of our control, because whether we like it or not, our brains may make us feel hungry, horny, hot, cold, sick, stressed, depressed, frustrated, insecure, jealous, nervous, anxious, awkward, afraid, ashamed, ugly, lonely, bored, disgusted, needy, greedy, angry, prejudice, hateful, and much more, towards every single thing we encounter in life, and we humans (as a whole) have been feeling these sensations since the beginning of time.

## How much $$$ to make these feelings go away?

A lot! Did you know that the pharmaceutical industry, as well as alcohol manufacturers and illegal drug cartels, make billions of dollars every single year from people trying to escape their natural, unwanted feelings?

And even still, as if we were on some sort of factory conveyor belt, humans commit suicide every forty seconds of every hour, every day, as a way to make these unwanted feelings go away.

**Born to feel a brain**

# CHAPTER 2

## I don't like my favorite thing anymore?

If you were to serve a person that was nearly starving to death their favorite food to eat, they would most likely be overjoyed with happiness. However, if you gave them that same meal everyday, three times a day for a month, they would most likely become, "sick of it."

This is how the human brain works: it's designed to make us spend the majority of our lives desperately wanting, sulking, and even obsessing over things we don't have, driving many insane with agonizing pain to the extent of lying, stealing, raping, and/or even killing for things it will later make them feel "sick of."

A terrible reality that leaves millions of humans bankrupt, divorced, imprisoned and dead every year, while pained from their brain to obtain the latest "thing."

For example, many professional athletes go broke within the first few years of retirement, just as many lottery winners are left broke within the first few years of receiving multi-millions of dollars in winnings.

This happens because, for many, life is not about being healthy, being safe, or even being alive: it's about serving a brain stimulation, regardless of whether it's good for us or bad: legal or illegal... leaves us dead, broke, or in jail.

# I don't like my favorite thing anymore?

The pain of wanting just might last forever yet the joy of having seems to be very short-lived for most...

So be prepared, because if you ever do end up buying the Ferrari of your dreams, you may be shocked to learn that within the first few days, hours, or in some cases even minutes of taking ownership, it will not make you feel happy.

And that's because all feelings come from the brain, not material objects, and so it will be entirely up to your brain's chemistry how much or how little of the "good-feeling sensations" you experience from the acquisition.

**This is usually when people** fall victim to the idea that buying more, perhaps in different colors, makes and/or models might do the trick (the same holds true with sexual partners), but in actuality, all we're really doing is "chasing a high" (searching for another hit), which is no different from what drug addicts do, because when the high of having goes away, the pain of wanting is what remains.

Everything we humans "really, really want" in life is not about making us happy, because to *want,* is to experience *absence*, which is a form of pain, thus making the true goal of "having," simply to stop wanting/obsessing.

Almost everything we humans do in life is to avoid pain...while many are notably driven insane...stealing and killing for items that are not perceived the same once obtained, attempting to satisfy the insatiable needs of their human brain.

So few of us ever catch on to the
cruel game from our brain.
Releasing insatiable needs to achieve that
for which we bleed,
just so that we somehow believe we succeed.
A feeling that is materialized by
individual items that later collect dust,
items that were once the obsession of our lust.
Things that made us say, "I won't stop till I bust"
are now thrown to the side by a brain
we can't trust.

**Born to feel a brain**

# CHAPTER 3

## A species driven by Pain?

250 million PAINKILLER prescriptions for opioids (heroin) are written every year, totaling $24 billion for the U.S. prescription PAINKILLER market. - CNBC

If there really were such a place as hell, I imagine PAIN would be the primary sensation driving it forward.

- Pain to eat: to the extent of killing billions of animals every single year for their meat, as we do

- Pain to have sex: to the extent of begging, masturbating, hiring prostitutes, and raping, as we do

- Pain to procreate: to the extent of artificially inseminating ourselves, as we do

- Pain to look youthful/beautiful: to the extent of undergoing life-threatening procedures, as we do

- Pain to have money: to the extent of stealing, dealing drugs, trafficking humans, robbing and killing for as little as pocket change, as we do

- Pain to serve a brain stimulation: to the extent of overdosing from drugs and alcohol, as we do

**Everything we cry for as children and spend our last dollars on as adults is meant to alleviate the pain from our brain.**

## A species driven by Pain?

If there really were such a place as hell, I imagine it would be designed in such a brilliant way that those condemned to experience it wouldn't even know they were in it.

Loss of hair, loss of teeth, loss of hearing, loss of eyesight, loss of bodily functions, loss of memory, loss of mind, and loss of life.

In natural order, I've been condemned to watch my parents deteriorate and die, then myself...weaken to the point where I can't chew food, see, hear, walk, move bowels, or even remember things anymore...helpless to defend myself or my loved ones, in a world that is known for abusing the weak.

## A species driven by Pain?

- **Without pain:** there would be no stimulus to fight, terrorize, or wage war

- **Without pain:** starvation, poverty nor disease would be detrimental

- **Without pain:** there would be no point in bullying or making fun of others

- **Without pain:** fear would not exist

- **Without pain:** there would be no such thing as "need," and without "need" (wants/desires), it is fair to say that the human species would cease to exist

**Thus making it very clear that PAIN is the primary sensation keeping our energy on this planet.**

We're the ones creating the world we live in, so as long as we continue to overpopulate and foster this impoverished system that breeds rape, murder, war, starvation, terrorism, drug abuse, human trafficking, home invasion, organ theft, genocide, incurable disease, enslavement, overpopulated prisons, concentration camps, homelessness, prostitution, mental illness (disorders, dementia, Alzheimer's), old age (disintegration) and now global warming, we'll continue to condemn ourselves to the very hell, we, as a whole, continue to create—in the name of pain.

To be happy we must be good, and we must realize that when one of us is hurting we're all hurting. Today, we're all witnessing a world that is at war—one that perpetuates hate and starvation in epic proportion. This isn't about electing better presidents, this is about correcting how we live and treat each other.

We mustn't allow pain to perpetuate and grow beyond the lengths it already has in this already very dangerous world.

Our energy is one—we've all been born under the same sun and therefore must have better plans in life than just equipping all people with guns.

**Born to feel a brain**

# CHAPTER 4

## Beware the Feelings Bitch

Feelings bitch: A person who is willing to hurt others and even themselves to serve "a brain" stimulation, doing things like:

- Molesting children

- Killing for material items

- Dog fighting

- Birthing crack-babies

- Trafficking humans

- Killing for insurance money

- Stealing organs from living bodies

- Polluting the environment for money

- Raising taxes to remove elderly people from their homes

- Waging war for land

- Legalizing deadly, addictive prescription medication

I oftentimes wonder, how many people have been killed for gold chains that weren't even real? #DontBeASlaveToABrain

**All of the ugly, evil, selfish, devastating actions displayed by man here on Earth exist only as they do because of the pain man is made to feel from a brain.**

*An idle brain causes pain (boredom, desperation, depravation, and insanity), which causes us to hurt each other.*

The weakest of us all are notably the most dangerous of us all: humans that do anything and everything they can to serve their brain stimulation, from sniffing paint to vandalizing, terrorizing, raping, and even killing innocent people for a thrill.

It needs to be made clear, once and for all, that hurting others and committing crimes does not make a person "gangster" (Scarface) but, rather, a slave to a brain that causes harm to others and even themselves for stimulation that never satisfies, only pacifies their human brain.

Do you realize that we live in a world where all we have to do is make it legal for people to kill each other, and then we do? Roughly one million Rwandan citizens were murdered after a radio announcement declared it legal to kill a select group of people—it was that easy! Can you believe it?

Information offers understanding, which at the highest level is limitless. I believe we'd do much better spending more on human development and less on weapons of mass destruction because we're a species capable of reaching the stars and perhaps even beyond...

**Born to feel a brain**

# CHAPTER 5

## MONEY

Born to work in a job-poor world. Does that sound right?

When a brain sounds off that piercing alarm in a person's stomach, letting them know it requires food (at least twice a day), they'll be made to feel pain. And for over one billion humans alive today, that means living in torture.

The punishment for not having money in this world is a slow, torturous death, passed down like a prison sentence to millions of humans every single year, <u>children not excluded</u>.

Which can only be described as diabolical because money does not extend to all humans in all parts of the world. Making it so that on this increasingly overpopulated planet, people are forcefully brought here solely to suffer.

Millions of impoverished children die within the first few days, months, and years of their lives, whereas many others are turned into desperate fiends—robbing, stealing, conning, corrupting, dealing drugs, stealing organs, trafficking humans, and killing for money.

**Which is exactly what is to be expected from a species that has to pay to make the pain from its brain go away.**

# MONEY

In America, this is **OUR NATIONAL DEBT**. Please pay close attention to the part that says, **"YOUR** *Family share"* because this is what YOU and YOUR family members owe:

Note: This figure increases by over $3-billion a day

Every paycheck you receive is taxed, every purchase you spend the remainder on is taxed, every year the property you own is taxed, and many (not all) of the people elected to control the money are corrupt and oftentimes eager to send our children to war—something is terribly wrong here.

The financial stability of our world depends greatly on the decisions made by our government and financial institutions, many of which make *poor decisions* on purpose, accruing trillions of dollars in debt, as a way to profit from the interest collected on the debt **(over $3-billion a day)**, interest that is to be paid to them by the working-class, the "middle-class" and their descendants through future taxation. This is an implementation of slavery that requires "middle-class-humans" and their unborn children to work an infinite amount of years in order to provide a steady flow of income to the wealthy, as the cost of goods and services continues to rise.

# MONEY

How many hours will you live, and how many of those hours will you need to exchange working for money to live?

Many people exchange more than forty hours of their lives every week for an amount of money that does not cover their living expenses.

**Forced to sleep when they are not tired and forced to wake up when they are not fully rested...**

Many of these people sacrifice their entire lives performing strenuous, backbreaking labor while conforming to the authority of others, all in the hopes of protecting their families from pain.

Most of them living with constant stress and the looming threat of their companies being downsized, moved overseas, and/or being completely replaced with computerized equipment, as the cost of goods and services continues to rise.

How can this world be good when it's set up like a game of Monopoly...one where you can only afford to go around the board so many times before a winner is declared and a loser is destroyed...one that turns neighbors into competitors and strangers into predators...one that starves millions of children to death every single year as punishment for not having money?

# MONEY

Record-store employees have been replaced by downloadable MP3 files, video-store employees have been replaced by streaming video, car factory employees have been replaced by giant mechanical arms, toll-booth employees have been replaced by computerized camera equipment, fast-food chains are installing kiosks and car manufacturers have successfully created self-operating vehicles, which may soon put millions of taxi drivers and delivery people out of work.

And since many wealthy people don't actually pay taxes because they're "smart" like Donald Trump, and "middle-class-humans" are being replaced by computerized equipment, I wonder who will pay the taxes that pave our streets, fund our schools, support our police officers, our firefighters, and programs like Medicaid and welfare that provide healthcare and food to children and families living under the poverty line?

The answer may be: No one, as "middle-class-humans" may be forced into a form of poverty where neither schools, peace officers, welfare, or health care exist. We have to be concerned that we live within a monetized world that is depending less and less on the billions of humans it has brought into existence to survive it. And I don't agree that we should be sending our children into a form of *hunger games,* where everyone is encouraged to bear arms—even on school grounds.

We must not birth a world of "poor-people" because they'll suffer, and we can't rely on or expect "the-worlds-richest-1%" to feed 7-billion children and growing.

# MONEY

I would like to empathize with the multi-billionaires of this world for a moment, using basketball as an example.

Have you ever seen a professional basketball team gain a huge lead on the opposing side, then suddenly start to lose on purpose because they felt bad for the losing team?

The answer is no, hells no! They're winning: why would anyone stop winning when they're in the lead?

Of course billionaires will attempt to buy politicians and do all they can to influence and manipulate laws that keep their businesses ahead.

If the goal in a capitalistic world is to be financially stable during our entire lifetime, and with the additional hopes of securing even our children's lives—why shouldn't billionaires do all they can to keep winning the game, especially when given the opportunity to buy and control the game themselves?

So what if, in this "game" over 1-billion humans currently live without food and clean water and so what if, billions more are soon born to experience the same, and so what if, **humans are the ones exposing the universe's energy to war, disease and famine?**

It's because if we don't aim to create a good, safe world for all, we'll be fostering a hellish environment, where one entity is the ruler, nothing is fair or equal, and the universe shall suffer this perpetuating destiny for all eternity.

As it stands, many rich-people have been able to avoid paying income taxes completely, and many have adopted to philosophies that include privatizing all schools, hospitals, and even roads, basically declaring war on poor people.

That is, until there's an actual war because that's when we're all made to believe we're "family," kindly asked and/or forcefully drafted to fight and even die for "our country."

Our time here on Earth can be compared to a blink of an eye when considering the distance of space between now and eternity. Therefore, we must think past these feelings we had no part in creating, ones that were obviously built for enslaving, if we are to align ourselves with good and evolve.

I'm pretty sure cavemen didn't think they needed to evolve, the same way I believe many people think we're perfect just as we are today.

However, according to our worldly statistics and the current state of our impoverished, violent world at war, the need for humans to evolve is too harsh of a fact to ignore because the suffering of our brothers & sisters has been happening in the billions! So yes, there is definitely need for improvement!

It is our responsibility as powerful, logical beings to correct the systematic errors we see perpetuating on Earth that negatively impact the source of our collective energy, by implementing systems of wellness. Ones that make our people laugh, not cry—expecting us to pay tolls on every street we drive.

**Born to feel a brain**

# CHAPTER 6

## "Dis-Orders" from the brain

* PTSD
* Anxiety
* Anorexia
* Depression
* OCD
* Necrophilia
* Cannibalism
* Separation anxiety
* Self-harm disorder
* Compulsive shopper
* Sleep terror disorder

* Bipolar
* Multiple personalities
* Pedophilia disorder
* Gender identity disorder
* Psychosis disorder
* Hypochondria
* Pica disorder
* Kleptomaniac
* Pyromaniac disorder
* Acute stress disorder
* Bestiality disorder

People aren't taught how to act when they have these "dis-orders," nor are they given a script or directed in any way. Yet, they display the same characteristics of every person that has ever had that same "dis-order," dating back thousands of years, and that's because "dis-orders" are nothing more than "orders" from a brain that is, statistically, one of many, outputting identical "dysfunctions."

Sensations from the brain are what determine our reality—they are what create perspective, they are what create opinions on life and of self, they are what enforce our fears and our fantasies, they are what make us who and what we are. From confident and brave to shy, timid, and afraid, we act how we feel, and what we're manufactured to feel has absolutely nothing to do with us!

## "Dis-Orders" from the brain.

I've seen kids smash their favorite video games to pieces just because they lost.

I've heard of parents shaking their babies to death just because they were crying.

I've heard stories of people killing each other from "road rage" just because of a traffic violation.

It's not who we are: it's what we are: under the command of a brain that can make us feel whatever we don't want, no matter how strong-minded we think ourselves to be...

Take Oprah Winfrey, for example. In 1981 she allegedly drove her car into a tree in an apparent suicide attempt after she found out that the man she loved was married with children.

Have you ever yelled at someone or thrown an object when feeling frustrated? Have you ever punched a wall, physically assaulted a person, or driven your car into a tree when forced to experience one of the many various sensations of pain from the brain?

If yes, then you already know just how powerful many of these "dis-orders" from the brain can actually be. Dictating our actions and thus the happenings of this world. Simply because we're led by sensations we do not control.

## "Dis-Orders" from the brain.

### End up in the wrong "hood" and you just might get shot!

When a brain is deprived of its desired foods and forced to dwell in a depressed environment that's run down with cracked streets, grime, and trash...where the homes are damaged with chipped paint, asbestos, mold, rats, and trillions of cockroaches, it's gonna release sensations of pain (frustration) so great that everyone in proximity will in one way or another be threatened with violence.

Making it so that in these parts of the world, fighting, rioting, theft, murder, and suicide are all very "normal," which is actually very "crazy!"

Humans have had to fight for their freedom since the beginning of time...

However, I believe the only fight for freedom we should've ever had is the one against our very own brains, because they are the ones enforcing upon us feelings of boredom, insecurity, anxiety, lust, disgust, prejudice, jealousy, frustration, greed, shame, anger, tension, fear, hate, and more...against others and even ourselves and, in almost all cases, for no reason at all!

**Born to feel a brain**

# CHAPTER 7

## So you wanna make a baby?

"Around the world, there are an estimated 17,900,000 orphans who have lost both parents and are living in orphanages or on the streets and lack the care and attention required for healthy development. These children are at risk for disease, malnutrition, and death." - Congressional Coalition on Adoption Institute (CCAI).

Is this really all it takes for children to be destroyed in this world—they just have to lose the protection of their parents? We really have to ask ourselves, "What kind of world are we forcing our children into?"

War on terror, war on drugs, human trafficking, organ theft, rape, starvation, home invasion, kidnapping, suicide, genocide, school shootings, public massacres, incurable diseases, false imprisonment, unemployment, foreclosure, raised taxes, devalued savings (inflation), poverty, famine, racism, enslavement, mental illness, murder, war, and death.

*This really doesn't seem like such a good place for children.*

Visited any good old-age homes lately? On record, thousands of nursing homes have been cited for abuse violations. Is this really what happens to people when they become too weak to defend themselves in this world—they get abused?

*This really doesn't seem like such a good place for elderly people either.*

Most people believe bringing a soul into this world is a "miracle." However, I wonder how many people alive today would actually want to come back here, knowing how this impoverished, overpopulated, overpriced, diseased world at war has been polluted to its destruction and is now facing global warming.

Coming back here would be like voluntarily boarding the Titanic, knowing it's going to sink, a terrible scenario that would subject us all to chaos, savagery, and death.

## So you wanna make a baby?

Bringing a child into this world means forcing them to face death at some point...are you sure you're okay with that?

The when, why, and how are what will remain a mystery until they are impacted with such a fate, which, for many, is gruesome, violent, and painful, if not, slow, old and dreadful.

When contemplating procreation, it is a must that we consider the result of death because it is imperative to understand the full nature of our creation, as well as the environment we're contributing our collective energy to.

That said, expecting parents should realize that they'll be implanting their children into an overpopulated environment that spends trillions of dollars on weapons of mass destruction, **weapons that were created to use against ourselves!**

And when I think about the humans who will inherit these weapons of mass destruction, from countries all around the world, in about 100 years from now, people who are not even born yet, people we know nothing of, I can't help but think, what the hell are we doing?

My mom once told me, "When a person makes a baby, an Angel from heaven is called down."
Well, since I now know that energy cannot be created or destroyed—only transferred, I'm starting to think that maybe my mom was onto something.

That said, I don't believe "Angels from Heaven" would want to be "called down" over and over again, just to be starved, raped, trafficked, impoverished, enslaved, diseased, disfigured, mentally impaired, sent to war to kill and/or be killed, billions of times for thousands of years and counting, all while having to serve a brain whatever kind of stimulation it requires, oftentimes illegal—in the hopes of avoiding its wrath of pain.

But maybe that's just me.

So, all things considered, can life be worth living when billions of people live solely to suffer, encapsulated within brains that require stimulation to the point of insanity, in an impoverished world where the feelings are for sale?

Perhaps maybe it is, but in order for us to evolve, questions like this must be asked because we must think logically if we are to arrive at greater levels of truth and understanding while experiencing these temporary lives here on Earth.

**Born to feel a brain**

# CHAPTER 8

## "Destiny"
## Has your life already been written?

We're about to explore what it means to be born into a life that has already been completely predetermined.

A baby girl named Bella was just born into a family in the Middle East. Bella's new family consists of a mother, father, uncle, and two brothers.

Her uncle has never been able to hold down a job, mostly because he suffers from sensations of laziness, forcing him to live in her family's home as a permanent guest.

No one knows it yet, but when Bella reaches twelve years old, her uncle will start to lust for her. His brain will release chemical sensations of desperation so great they can actually be compared to starvation, and so in an effort to quiet this tormenting pain from his brain, he decides to rape Bella.

Once the news gets out of what Bella's uncle has done, her family will join together with friends and neighbors, drag Bella out into the street, and proceed to strike her head, face, and body with rocks and stones until she is pronounced dead.

This is what is known as an, "honor killing." Bella has been accused of dishonoring her family for getting raped, and so they justify killing her as a way to preserve their honor.

It should be clear to us all that Bella did not choose the family or religion she would be born into, nor did she have any control over her looks or the gender she would assume upon entering this world.

A beautiful girl was born into a family with a rapist; a family that believes girls should be murdered for getting raped.

Thus making this a predetermined destiny that has already played out millions of times, killing millions of little girls, and understanding how human brains may force upon us sensations of desperate desire, lust, disgust, greed, shame, fear, and anger tells us exactly why this world continues to suffer year after year, without any end currently in sight.

## "Destiny"
## Has your life already been written?

Who will our parents be, and what will our lives be like upon entering their home?

Are your parents mentally ill? Are they physically or sexually abusive? Are they drug addicts or drug dealers? Are they extremely religious, forcing you to live an odd, uncomfortable lifestyle? Do your parents harm you over every little mistake you make? Did your parents deliver you into a life in which you experience starvation daily?

The lives we're "born to feel" will have very little to do with us and everything to do with the parents who claim us, the environment we're delivered into, the gender we identify with, and the brain type we assume...and for many, this means "serving" a lifetime of pain and confusion.

- Be born in Ethiopia, and you just might starve and dehydrate to death before getting eaten by vultures.

- Be born in India, and your parents just might cut off your hands and feet to gain sympathy from tourists when begging for money.

- Be born to a mother who refuses to give up cigarettes, drugs, and/or alcohol during her pregnancy, and you just might end up going through life being ridiculed and rejected for being a "disfigured freak show."

- Be born mentally ill, and you just might live out your entire life experiencing false perceptions and hallucinations from your brain, wrapped in straitjackets, strapped to tables, and trapped till death. Very possibly abused routinely, sexually and/or physically, by the people employed to "care" for you.

- Be born in a third-world country where neither fairness nor opportunity exist, and you just might end up going through life treated as property...bought, sold and traded for sex, labor and game.

- Be born with HIV/AIDS or cancer, and you just might end up dying before the age of ten years old, living out your entire life in hospitals, overwhelmed with sensations of fear, worry, and pain.

- Be born in the wrong neighborhood, and you just might get shot for wearing the wrong color.

Already, billions of humans have lived solely to experience such ill fates, while billions more await the same—all created by the human brain.

## "Destiny"
## Has your life already been written?

Once a politician is elected into power, they're permitted to spend tax dollars on our behalf by assigning work contracts to companies that provide services.

The only problem with this is that many politicians abuse this responsibility by funding unjust, redundant programs run by companies that they own, in part, or receive generous contributions (campaign money) from.

In fact, many politicians have gone as far as waging wars just so they can charge taxpayers billions of dollars on supplies they earn revenue from—a scheme that claims the lives of millions of people each time it is put into effect.

This is what happens when weak people are put in charge of spending billions of dollars on our behalf: they literally kill for it while creating a world at war that affects the destinies of us all!

**Warning: Humans must not be incentivized to make money from people dying in combat, because they will! Nobody should be allowed to make money from war. Period.**

As a child, I believed politicians were more like angels who safeguarded us from harm, not fiends that spent their days figuring out how to siphon dollars that in turn contribute to the perpetuating destiny of our world to be what it is today, unsafe.

**However, I do <u>NOT</u> blame government officials for the current state of our world...**

Because as long as there are pregnant women willing to destroy themselves and the children they carry within them to serve their brain a cigarette, it should come as no surprise to us that there are humans in power willing to destroy strangers to serve their brain billions of dollars...

- Causing economic depressions

- Starting wars that claim the lives of millions

- Destroying the environment with pollution

- Contaminating water supplies

- Attempting to get all people addicted to legal and/or illegal drugs

- Trafficking humans

These are not problems created by politicians: these are problems created by humans that are pained by their brain to deliver any kind of stimulation they can find, continuously affecting the destiny of this entire world since the beginning of time.

## "Destiny"
## Has your life already been written?

Can you imagine what the destiny of humankind will be when we start feeling the effects of global warming?

As the Earth warms, plants, vegetables, and fruits will start to die. Having lost their food supply, all Earth's wildlife will die as well.

Once our plants, fruits, vegetables and animals start to die, there will be over seven billion humans living in complete chaos, pillaging and killing in an effort to avoid pain while slowly dying from a lack of resources.

Many of the companies responsible for causing this harm to the world today work tirelessly with the government to stop new laws and regulations—affecting the destiny of this planet and every single thing on it.

**Born to feel a brain**

# CHAPTER 9

## Don't lie to me!

I'm fat, I'm ugly, nobody loves me, I need more cake, I need another cigarette, I need more beer, I need more drugs, I need to rape, I need to hurt, I need to kill, buying those shoes will make me happy, getting bigger boobs will make me happy, leasing that car will make me happy, cheating on my spouse will make me happy...

Are all commonly **FELT** lies! The biggest liar of all: the human brain! It enforces lies through the most powerful, most convincing method of all: feelings

Every time you do something new or have a significant new thought, your brain creates a neural pathway. This looks like a little electric string that connects to the newly stored information.

The first time a person tries to stand, walk, ride a bicycle, color within the lines, use a fork and knife etc. they're likely to be shaky and unstable. This happens because the electric string (neural pathway) they're trying to establish is weak at first.

However, each time the thought or action is revisited, the string gets thicker and stronger, allowing us to become more comfortable with the information and practices thereof. This is what allows us to function and operate as we do, without having to relearn everything every day.

"Practice makes perfect."

**Warning**: Parents are responsible for creating neural pathways in their children's brains!

Tragically, many parents create entire fields of neural pathways in their children's brains that are based on false information—either on purpose or because of ignorance and/or just plain laziness.

In fact, most parents seem perfectly fine with making their children believe Santa Claus and the Tooth Fairy are watching them and may enter their homes, undetected and unannounced, to bring gifts or take a tooth, based on their behavior.

Truth is light that offers clarity to see further into what truly matters. The closer we get to truth, the closer we get to purpose. Lies are clutter in the mind, confusion that exists solely to keep people eternally lost and away from what is good and right in life.

If children knew Santa Claus wasn't the one bringing them gifts, they might appreciate their parents more—realizing that the gifts they receive are a result of their parents hard work, sacrifice, and love, not "free stuff" from a magical stranger.

**Furthermore, it should be firmly understood that the process of giving is not the responsibility of "others" but in fact our very own, and if we are to have a "good world," then it is completely up to us to make it that way, not something or someone else's!**

Hard work, sacrifice, and a driving force called love are what children should be made to understand as soon as possible, so they may develop and nurture powerful neural pathways that are based on truth and good, not confusion and lies.

Our goal should be to establish the purest field of neural pathways possible—a place that is free and clear of impurities, a place where positive thoughts can exist, prosper, and evolve into action.

# Don't lie to me!

There were liars that made others believe African American's were less than human and should be treated as animals with no souls—born to be enslaved, tortured, and starved by those who claimed to be superior. These lies caused millions of beautiful, good-hearted men, women, and children to experience hell on Earth.

There were liars that made others believe Jewish people were evil and therefore should be imprisoned, starved, tortured, gassed, burned, and buried alive, side by side with their children. These lies caused millions of innocent, good-hearted men, women, and children to experience hell on Earth.

There were liars that started wars, claiming the opposing side had "weapons of mass destruction," with the intent to destroy. These lies caused hundreds of thousands of innocent men, women, and children to be destroyed as bombs were randomly dropped on their villages.

How can peace exist when there are such powerful, manipulative liars that can so easily sway our thoughts and actions?

It can exist simply by knowing and showing others that goodness is the most powerful way of life and cannot be achieved by lying or supporting evil actions, such as war.

Unless such war is in self-defense only, carefully aimed directly at those who pose true threat.

## Don't lie to me!

Religion is one of the first big businesses ever to be invented and one of the worst widespread lies to ever be believed.

These groups fought to amass the most "followers" in order to gain the most control. *It's diabolical how much blood has been spilled on Earth's soil in the name of religion.*

Billions of humans never searched for their own ideas in life because they were forced to inherit beliefs from birth that were created solely to control people like robots.

How can humans evolve when so many live according to books that were passed down by people that believed:

- Women should not have equal rights

- Enslaving humans is justifiable

- Homosexuals should be destroyed and burn for eternity in hell

- People guilty of petty crimes should be stoned, hung, or decapitated in public

- Cutting off the hands of a starving child for stealing an apple is justifiable

- Executing women for dating outside their appointed religion is justifiable

- Selling infant girls as wives is justifiable

Thousands of years and billions of people later—still not evolving because they continue to follow "scripts" on how to live and think while threatened with being condemned to hell for having a unique thought.

One of the biggest lies of all stole away people's right to think for themselves while sending them to fight wars to kill and/or be killed.

In my opinion, believing in God as the almighty source of goodness and positivity is magnificent. However, I believe following books and dictators that suggest people should be hurt, sent to death, and burn for eternity in hell for living free, nonviolent lives is pure evil.

There's no better way to separate humanity than to make us believe we're all different. #endreligion in the most honorable way possible so that "the future" may actually have a "new day," one that does not reflect the actions of others but, rather defines us all as brothers.

**Born to feel a brain**

# CHAPTER 10

## Judge-less

Fact: We humans don't control what "turns us on" or what "turns us off." We'll either be made to want something—in some cases, so <u>desperately</u> that we're made to behave like "crack-head" fiends for it—or want nothing to do with it, so painfully that we're made to express <u>disgust</u> while pushing it away.

For example,

- We may <u>see</u> an attractive person and <u>feel</u> a need for their affection, or we may <u>see</u> an ugly person and <u>feel</u> disgusted.

- We may <u>smell</u> a fragrance and <u>feel</u> a need to buy the bottle, or we may <u>smell</u> a fart and <u>feel</u> disgusted.

- We may <u>touch</u> something voluptuous and <u>feel</u> turned on, or we may <u>touch</u> something dirty and <u>feel</u> disgusted.

- We may <u>hear</u> a song and <u>feel</u> a need to purchase the album, or we may <u>hear</u> an alarm clock and <u>feel</u> disgusted.

- We may <u>taste</u> delicious foods and <u>feel</u> the need to eat until we're bloated, or we may <u>taste</u> something gross and <u>feel</u> disgusted.

This is why so many people express disgust (to the extent of cruelty) toward people with Down syndrome "Retards," and toward people who are obese, disfigured, of different races, of different creeds, of different sexual orientation, and those who are considered old and unattractive.

The truth is that many people feel unwanted sensations of disgust toward most things they encounter in life, including themselves.

Pay attention to how "ugly" this really gets: when a brain observes its own physical form, for instance, in a mirror, it's not uncommon for it to unleash chemical sensations of disgust, insecurity, depression, frustration, or even hate to the extent of suicide... #You-big-nose-pimple-face-fatso!

Oh, snap! No wonder why this world is filled with hate crimes, racism, war, genocide, suicide, and all the other evil shit that happens multiple times within each hour of every day that passes. It's because humans are at the mercy of a brain that may not only make them feel disgust and hatred toward others, but even toward themselves! This has to stop.

We owe it to ourselves—us, we, the human family—to never see race, religion, sexual orientation, or appearance as a way to judge others again but, rather, understand all humans by way of what we've all been born to feel and empathize!

Guaranteeing our thoughts and intentions are always pure and without prejudice, judgment and hate. Upheld by the irrefutable logic that we're all the same...

**Born to feel a brain**

# CHAPTER 11

## Why the Hell does that feel good, brain?

Throwing eggs at an old man, dropping water balloons on random people, bullying, raping, humiliating, vandalizing, and even killing for pleasure all have one thing in common...

The perpetrators in these examples are all motivated by the "good-feeling" sensations they receive from their brain when their victims are forced to feel fear, discomfort, and pain.

Which basically means that people do bad things because their brain rewards them for it:

### Human suffering stimulates the human brain

When I was in my teens, a man once told me how he and his friends put a firecracker up a cat's ass, and how funny it was to see the cat running in fear just before the blast.

Stories like these are often told with enthusiasm and received well with laughs, and that's because stories like these are what trigger deprived brains to stop releasing sensations of pain.

I recently saw a video of a sixty-eight-year-old woman being verbally abused by teens on a school bus. They called her fat, old, gross, disgusting, poor, and more, bringing her to tears, which only made them laugh harder.

We need to understand that hurting and degrading others for a thrill is not funny or cool but, rather, the work of unevolved individuals who are enslaved by the pain from their brain. Blind to the fact that what they're doing is wrong because their brains **make them feel** "it's all right."

Approximately ten million people saw the video of the sixty-eight-year-old woman being verbally abused and raised hundreds of thousands of dollars for her.

I like to believe that humans will soon evolve to a much greater level because, through the power of technology and social media, we're now able to see and "share" the happenings of this world like never before, creating a perfect "network" of awareness that could lead to compassion, advocacy, and a level of understanding that may ultimately unify us all as one.

Good is the greatest of all other possibilities and what is necessary to achieve peace for all. It should be deeply felt that we are inexplicably lucky that goodness continues to exist in our world, and it should be firmly understood that we are solely responsible for preserving this amazing greatness.

However, if we, as a whole, fail to define ourselves as good, we'll continue to be a species in distress, overpopulating prisons in this overpopulated, impoverished world at war that is in motion to destroy all.

**Born to feel a brain**

# CHAPTER 12

## Of course there's a Hell

**If that which we do not see would make us cry, does that mean when we laugh we live a lie?**

Did you know that in exchange for a five-second orgasm, humans sentence millions of babies to death in a blistering hot desert without food or water every single year like clockwork? Many eaten by vultures the moment their depleted bodies become too weak to move or defend themselves.

There's a place that exists in clear sight today, a blistering hot place where humans are brought solely to starve and be eaten by vultures—a place where humans are the food! Can anyone describe a more accurate description of hell?

**Fact: Energy cannot be created or destroyed, which means the energy that occupies our temporary bodies was not created by our parents but, rather, transferred from some unknown origin.**

If there really is such a place as heaven, and we're all from there, as so many people seem to believe, the most selfish (hellish) act I could ever imagine would be one that forces a soul from Heaven to live a condemned life in exchange for a five-second orgasm...a fleeting feeling from the brain.

**Born to feel a brain**

# CHAPTER 13

## Stealing Heaven

Are temporary humans creating life or trapping energy?

The late Steve Jobs, former CEO of Apple, said, "Everyone wants to go to heaven, but no one wants to die to get there."

To that, I ask: Why do all these people who want to be in heaven continue to make babies in an overpopulated, overpriced, diseased, violent world at war from which we must all die?

*Energy cannot be created or destroyed, which means the energy that occupies our bodies was not created by our parents but, rather, transferred from some unknown origin.*

It is for this reason that I believe in the soul, the energy, far more than I could ever believe in the body. The body is made up of around 90% bacteria, hosts around one hundred trillion bacteria cells, and is simply not built to last.

Billions are born sick, disfigured, and mentally ill, dying in as little as hours, days, weeks, months, and years, whereas energy can never be destroyed.

Imagine, for a moment, that there is a God, and you are able to see what God sees…your children raped, murdered, starved, and diseased, every second of every day. All while more of your children are brought in to experience the same perpetuating destiny, year after year, for thousands of years and counting...

**All because sex is perceived as an irresistible sensation from the brain.**

## Stealing Heaven

As a child, I attended Catholic Church a few times, never regularly or with any conviction: it just depended on who was taking care of me at the time.

I dreaded the days; the experience was always boring and difficult to sit through, not to mention I never really understood what anyone was saying or what was going on.

Years later, when I was around twenty-two years old, I was visiting with relatives who had plans to attend evening mass. Although I really didn't care to go, I decided to join them out of respect.

When I got there, I noticed that the church was different from any others I had ever been to before. There were no rituals or moments where people had to stand and chant in unison, and the priest was well spoken and did a decent job of connecting with his audience.

He told us the story of Adam and Eve. I was captivated by his story, and so I shall tell it now in my own words.

Adam and Eve were placed on Earth by God and given everything they needed to live in peace with one another. There was no harsh weather to bear or things to fear, no boredom, pain, or sickness to feel.

The only request God had in exchange for their eternal peace was that they were never to eat the "forbidden fruit" from the "tree of life," which would ultimately give them the power to create life themselves.

Note: I interpreted the "forbidden fruit" as having sex, mainly because the "tree of life" was said to offer the power to create life. However, I in no way wish to offend anyone or insist that my understanding of the "forbidden fruit" or the "tree of life" are as I interpreted them to be.

I neither study nor practice religion.

On with the story…

Adam and Eve understood full well that they were not to eat the "forbidden fruit," as this would hurt God greatly and bring darkness to his light. And because they loved him so, they agreed never to do such a thing.

That was until they met Lucifer, the devil. He was not frightening or scary toward them at all but seemingly kind and rather informative.

He told the two that the only reason God did not want them to eat the "forbidden fruit" was because God did not want them to share in his great powers to create life—making it seem as if God were denying them the greatest gift of all.

Adam and Eve were enchanted by the thought of possessing such great powers, and like most humans who cannot resist temptation, they decided to feel what it would be like to have sex and create life, and so they did.

God soon appeared and said something to the effect of:

You have broken our trust and have done exactly what I asked you never to do...hurting me to an extent that you may never know, and so I must now leave you. Please be aware that because of what you have done, the energy that once protected you from pain, fear, and sickness shall no longer be present because you have destroyed it.

Adam and Eve were saddened by this information and began to feel remorse and fear for the first time in their lives.

Eve also began to feel pain and various sensations of sickness throughout her pregnancy, which only got worse on the day of delivery, causing her to let out screams that made it seem as if she were dying.

And the pain seemed to be just as excruciating for their baby too, because it also let out horrible screams upon entering the world and continued on like that for months to come.

The rest is said to be history to the present time.

Unless I completely misinterpreted the priest's story, what I found to be most interesting about it was that it basically said procreation was not God's will but, rather, the work of Lucifer, the devil, which confused me because it has always been my understanding that the Catholic Church encourages its followers to birth as many babies as they can.

In fact, that's the one thing I understand most, if not all, religions have in common: is that they encourage their followers to birth as many babies as they can, providing them with more followers/soldiers, in the hopes of gaining total control.

However, it never really worked out that way for any religion because, in actuality, the only thing birthing more people has ever done is create bigger wars with billions of more starving mouths to feed.

That said, I decided to give further consideration to the priest's story and the possibility of our existence on this planet being the plan of Lucifer, the devil.

*Note: The following is just food for thought and should not be taken as fact by any means.*

I found that the best way to analyze this story would be to find conflicting information that disproved it, as well as supporting information that gave it validity.

To disprove this story, I entertained the theory that humans evolved from monkeys.

However, I have a major problem with this theory because monkeys still exist today: however, humans aren't spawning from them.

I see monkeys, and I see humans, but I don't see anything in the middle. Where did all the middlemen go, the "missing links" and why has the process of middlemen evolving from monkeys stopped, if there was ever such a process to begin with?

There's obviously something missing here: therefore, I'm not entirely satisfied with this theory of how humankind came to be.

Next was to try and understand why God wouldn't want humans to create life on their own...why would such a great, all-knowing entity of goodness be against this?

I searched high and low for an answer that made sense to me, and that's when I discovered the history of humankind—creating wars, enslaving, raping, torturing, hanging, beheading, disemboweling, castrating, burning, and burying each other alive throughout our entire human history.

- I learned that over one billion souls and counting live in diseased-infested lands with no clean water to drink.

- I learned that within seconds of each hour that passes, people rape, rob, and kill one another every single day like clockwork.

- I learned that millions of children die from starvation and/or dehydration every single year. Many eaten by vultures the moment their depleted bodies become too weak to move or defend themselves.

- I learned that billions of animals are slaughtered in the cruelest forms imaginable for fur, meat, and game every single year.

And most importantly, I learned that behind it all is a human brain, designed to drive most insane with pain just for having to sit in one spot for too long...undoubtedly making this a slave system.

**Leaving me to ask, "Why would God want us to create life on our own, knowing how irresponsible we would be at overpopulating this planet with suffering souls, to its destruction and our demise?"**

Now science: Human pollution is causing Global warming, which is apparently going to dry up all of Earth's water and crops, turning humans into savages until nothing remains, forcing humans to die agonizing deaths from a lack of resources...a scenario that ends with Earth being engulfed in fire, which, interestingly enough, is allegedly the devil's favorite scenario.

So according to the science of global warming, all humans will inevitably die in a state of suffering, while Earth slowly becomes a big ball of fire...

That definitely sounds like hell to me, one that God would certainly want to protect his children from—his energy from.

That said, it should be understood that this was just a story I tried to make sense of. **I'm neither religious nor a scientist, and therefore do not have any concrete evidence that points to Earth's absolute destruction.**

I simply suggest we use our powerful brains to consider what life for humans will be like on Earth, as the human population grows from 7 billion polluting bodies to over 10 billion polluting bodies by the end of the century, and already **one billion** of us do not have food or clean, drinkable water, and are still warring over things like race—the color of our skin.

## Stealing Heaven

When asked, how do you feel when you think about the families of the people you've shot dead? This very young gangbanger (gun-man) replied, "I try not to *think* about stuff like that."

Unfortunately for our world, *thinking* is not a requirement and that's because humans can survive solely by reacting to the sensations from their brain, and sadly, most don't challenge what they *feel,* not even when what they *feel* is to rape, rob, kidnap and/or kill.

Some may ask: why not rape, rob, kidnap, and/or kill? Why not beat and bully those that are weaker? Why not approve and/or sell products that cause cancer? Why not wage wars for personal gain? We all have to die anyway, right?

The answer is clear: all humans are made of energy, and all energy is connected as one. This means WE ARE ONE, and would still be unified as one whether present on this planet or elsewhere...

**And this is where I believe we find "God." Not as a biblical figure or bearded man in space but, rather, the energy that is within us all, joining us as one.**

It is understood that the more energy something possesses, the stronger it is, and the further it can reach. So with that said, it should be understood that the more good we aim to create ourselves by caring for and empathizing with one another, the closer to each other we will become, and the stronger our energy will be as one.

We must realize that hate and evil are weaknesses of the mind, and although evil is often glorified as strength, it should finally be understood—once and for all—as weakness because evil is a reaction of pain from the brain. Therefore, defining evil people as those who live in pain from their brain, which in effect is weakness.

Conversely, good is a controlled state of mind, one that empowers us to live beyond the insatiable needs our brains impose upon us, thus allowing us to evolve from the ruins they've created.

We need to realize that no matter how much we work for, steal for, and even kill for material items, we'll be leaving it all behind for others—even the stuff we burry, because everything we do is for the future. Everything we touch gets left behind! Therefore, everything we do should be in the name of peace and prosperity for all, by way of truth and understanding of all.

We must think selflessly, not selfishly, by planting seeds we can all eat from in our next lives. Share love, share wealth, share knowledge, and our energy will prosper because the meaning of life is for us all to evolve as one, just as we've been doing from the days of cavemen.

This starts by acknowledging and intensely caring that today, millions of children are born to starve every single year like clockwork, and over one billion humans do not have access to clean drinking water—a perpetuating destiny that affects millions of souls every year, which clearly, sooner or later—will affect us all—because energy cannot be created or destroyed, only transferred, which puts us all in line to live and feel as these souls do, in due time.

The sin that would ensure this fate would be our apathetic, dispassionate, uninterested attitude toward our brothers and sisters, our energy—ourselves. Making it so that there would be no difference in being next in line to experience this horrible fate. Because again, we're all made of energy, and therefore can be encapsulated as one of these souls at any time we are decapsulated from our current "selves."

To live in a good world, we must care for and help others by creating systems of wellness, the same way that so many of us hope and believe God, as man or spirit, would do for us.

I believe that to experience God on Earth, we have to unlock God within ourselves, by first understanding the sensations that cause us harm. Sensations that have been stemming from mankind since the beginning of man's time—from our fathers to our children, that are now multiplying by the billions, creating "our future" and welcoming the new into a reality that breeds hate, thrives on war and experiences disease and starvation in epic proportion.

We must not leave this world behind, as it is, and always has been since the beginning of our time—suffering from the insatiable needs of mankind.

With all my love and hope for a better tomorrow,

Mighty Angel
"In Gods Hands"